The Blueprint

Strategies to Building a Successful Real Estate Business

David Adam Kurz

Rudy Hernandez

The Blueprint

Printed by:
CreateSpace Independent Publishing Platform

Published in the United States of America

Book ID: 160912-00537

ISBN-13: 978-1546632764
ISBN-10: 154663276X

Here's What's Inside...

Dedication

*To the woman who has given me unconditional
love and support, My Amazing Mother.
To the woman who encourages me daily with love
and support, my beautiful fiancé.
To the Kurz Team. Without your trust and
dedication, I would not be here today.
To my daughters, Olivia and Amber for supporting
Daddy with ever move he makes.*
~ David

*To my mother Petra, my first teacher in life.
To my amazing sisters Ivy, Janet and Claudette,
thank you for showing the importance of having a
purpose.
To the Nu World Title family, I am eternally
grateful to each of you.
To my beautiful wife and son, Myriam and Dylan.
You two are my world.*
~ Rudy

Introduction

Have you ever wondered what separates real estate agents and professionals who are widely successful to those who can't string more than a few deals together in a year? What does the successful agent know compared to those who are new to the industry?

We are tired of watching agents enter the business excited to become agents, but six months later, they are back at their day job because they could never acquire a real estate transaction.

The truth is that owning a home is part of the American Dream. People need the help of dedicated, passionate agents to help them realize that dream. We want every agent to be equipped with the tools they need to have phenomenal success, even if they are brand new to the industry or have only closed a few transactions. We believe you have unique talents to share with the world. There is only one you. Our goal with this book is to help you see how you can put yourself out into the world in a very big way, so that you can help more people realize their own American Dream.

There is nothing more satisfying than sitting with agents and helping them grow their business.

The material we are going to share with you in this book is from years spent being a real estate agent and then learning how to grow a successful team. This is a win-win for all of us. The more involved we are with our team members in their growth, the stronger their business becomes. This book is our gift back to the industry we love. We want every new agent or every agent who is thinking about leaving the business or frustrated with not making more money to have the knowledge and tools needed to achieve success.

Enjoy the book!

We hope this book inspires you to live your dreams. Don't settle for just average. Go for it! We are here to support you to be more successful than you ever thought possible. You deserve to live the lifestyle you want to live.

To Your Success!

David Adam Kurz & Rudy Hernandez

The Beginning:
It's Been Done Before

Susan: Good afternoon, this is Susan Austin, and I'm excited to be here with David Kurz and Rudy Hernandez. David and Rudy are going to be sharing with us their strategies for building a successful real estate business. Welcome, guys!

Rudy: We are excited to be here, Susan.

Susan: Why do you think so many real estate agents struggle to build successful real estate businesses?

David: We titled this book *The Blueprint*. It's about developing the foundation of understanding what it means to build a real estate company when you first get into the business.

A lot of people join the real estate business—title companies, mortgage brokers, etc.—thinking they're going to have success overnight. They don't understand that without a solid foundation, they can't take the future steps forward to get to the money they intend to make. The good news is that this blueprint is based on the fact that other agents have done this many times before.

There are people who are already very successful in this business; in fact, they're much more successful than we are. So please know building a successful real estate business has been done before. You don't have to reinvent the wheel and because everybody is a little bit different, which is what makes you stand out, you can do things your own way—as long as you follow the blueprint from the very beginning.

Rudy: One of the true statistics about the real estate business is that 10% of any real estate company's agents are always the producing agents. This means the other 90% are not producers. There's a reason this statistic holds true for every real estate company out there. The 90% don't understand the blueprint for success. This book hopes to solve that. This is for those 90% who aren't having the success they want.

David: Many real estate agents don't realize how hard it is to be a real estate agent. It seems easy at first glance - stage a house for sale, put up a sign, and watch the offers come flying through the door. Since they don't develop the foundation necessary to build a successful business, they become accidental agents; or what I call "secret agents" because they do not promote themselves well. Nobody knows they exist.

They're in a position where they've sold their cousin and their brother a house, and now they have nowhere to turn. They don't know what else to do. They get frustrated, and when they get frustrated, they give up on the business or they just become fly-by-night realtors, saying, "Whatever falls in my lap, I'll take it because I just don't know what else to do." This thinking can often cause them to leave the business, which is what we want to help prevent.

Rudy: Why don't we take a moment and outline briefly exactly what it is a real estate agent does? Someone hears *REALTOR*, and they think you're just trying to sell real estate. However there's a lot more to it, and I think if we break it down to its core, it will make it easier to have a full grasp and understanding of what an agent is supposed to be doing.

David: Great idea, Rudy. You can't talk about a REALTOR without mentioning being a negotiator. In order to be a good negotiator, you have to be able to understand, read, and write real estate contracts.

When you work with both buyers and sellers, you must be able to work with different personalities.

A REALTOR also has to be a market consultant, which enables you to advise your clients on market conditions, prices, mortgages, legal requirements, and related matters.
Then of course, you need to be a marketing specialist and use that to leverage yourself, at the very minimum.

In addition to hosting open houses and participating in network events, you must prepare contracts and purchase agreements, work with title companies like Rudy's title company, Nu World Title, and understand what is the purpose of an escrow.

You also have to know the responsibility you have as a real estate agent and the legal conditions you have to follow, maintain specific timelines, oversee the entire timeline of a contract and the disbursement of funds.

Speaking of funds, you must be able to understand a buyer's needs and financial resources by working with the right lender who can understand what a buyer's capability is. This is all just the tip of the iceberg.

Susan: There's a lot more to it than just getting in your car, driving around, and showing people pretty houses.

Rudy: That's the perception, right?

David: This perception gets even more diluted when you watch TV shows that depict a multi-billionaire landing in a private jet, picking the agent up in a Rolls Royce, who then sells them a $20 million house in the heart of Miami. Then, of course, all their friends are going to call the agent, as well.

People get into the business thinking it's an instant get-rich-quick scheme, and the truth is that it's not. It takes a lot of hard work and dedication.

Susan: They don't show on TV how you can show one buyer 40 homes before they even make an offer.

David: They only see the success, the end result. They don't see the journey to success. When people fall into this specific journey, it's a difficult one, and they tend to go down the wrong path. They haven't laid down the foundation and I think this is what it's all about: having the blueprint so you can lay that foundation.

Lead Flow: How Important Is Initial Lead Flow and Where Do They Come From

Susan: Let's talk about how important is it for a new agent to have leads? Do you need to have a database of 1,000 people to be successful in this business?

Rudy: A lead is what you perceive it to be. Leads are all around us. A lead can be a person you buy from at the grocery store. When you define a lead, there are leads everywhere, meaning a lead is a human being who has a job and the capability to purchase or sell a home.

David: Then on the same note, the very first place anyone is ever going to look for a lead is their intimate circle or sphere of influence.

Rudy: You'd be surprised though, not everyone does that.

David: You're right. Usually, when an agent asks me, "Where do I get leads," I say, "You have a whole bunch of them in your pocket right now."

They respond, "What are you talking about?"

I tell them, "Give me your cell phone. How many contacts do you have in here? This is your initial lead base."

Your initial lead base will begin with doing good work for a few people and in turn getting some referrals from those few people. Over time, you can develop a referral-based business, which is ultimately what you want. You want to be able to market yourself, but not make it necessary. You market to stay in people's minds, but it's not necessary because 90% to 100% of your business will become a referral-based business. As a brand new agent, your initial lead base is in your telephone, which is exactly where you should start.

Rudy: In my opinion, your lead base is everywhere you go throughout your week in the normal course of your everyday life, but your telephone is a pretty good place to start.

David: I agree, Rudy. You want to develop the ability to speak to anyone around you. If you don't have a big lead base in your telephone, then you want to reach out to your inner sphere of influence. Your closest friends and family can become your initial cheerleaders. They tell their friends and family about you and now your sphere of influence grows from maybe five or six people to 15 to 20 people. Through word of mouth, you continue to grow and grow.

Susan: Are there ways to get continuous leads?

David: Of course, there are. From social media, or you can pay for them through paid lead sources. However, as Rudy said, you can get them at the grocery store, when you pick up your laundry, or when you go out to eat. There are leads everywhere. You just need to be open to finding them.

Rudy: You can also use third party vendors.

David: There are a million different ways to get leads. As a new agent, do you need leads? Is it important? Of course it is. It's very important to get leads, but you can develop those leads slowly by starting in your initial sphere of influence.

You begin by calling every single person in your phone and saying, "Hey, I'm a real estate professional. This is what I do for a living. I need you to help me by either buying or selling a house with me or by telling someone else what I do and keeping me in mind." You would be surprised how successful just making those calls can be. That's your initial database.

Then you grow your database by doing all the free things you can possibly do. Build a strong social media presence. Door-knock in a neighborhood you want to farm. Have consistent meetings with people around you.

Talk to everyone around you. Go to networking events. Don't become a hermit. Go out and talk to people.

Let me tell you why networking events are important. Other people will say you should not go to networking events with people in your same career path because they're not a lead source for you. That's absurd. While that may be the case in some other cities, somewhere likes Miami where the city is completely divided up is a whole different story.

If I go to a networking event right now in the heart of Miami and I need an agent who works in Fort Lauderdale, Palm Beach, Aventura, Southwest Ranches, or Miramar, these places are an hour and a half in traffic for me. If I get a buyer and seller in those areas, they are now a network person who I can call for a referral. Do not look at your fellow agents as the competition. Look at them as potential referral source.

We'll get into this in more detail later in the book, but just remember your leads are everyone you know and everyone they know. It's important to consistently speak to people everywhere around you.

Getting involved in charity events, and other activities you actually care about, is another great way to get more leads.

However, don't just join a charity because you want to get leads out of it. You're joining a charity because you care. You're going to do it long-term, and people will begin to trust you over time.

Rudy: Become a walking billboard. Don't be a secret.

Getting Past Your Sphere of Influence: Other Avenues of Approach

David: Let me share with you the story of Eric Morales. Eric joined our company less than a year ago in November. He really starts doing real estate work in January. He goes all-in. He listens to everything I tell him to do, he focuses on his sphere of influence; his sphere of influence then leads him to more leads, which then leads to more leads. Eric completes two or three new development deals, which have put him on the map. Those new development deals are paying him a significant 10% commission. Now we're talking about an agent who's probably going to do $500,000 in commission in his first year in real estate.

I tell this story because I want people to understand they can do it as long as they stay focused, begin with their sphere of influence and have continuous and rigorous follow-up. Eric did all that. Of course, without the follow-up, none of those people would have worked with him. Some people took sometimes three or four months to even say, "Fine, let's go look at the place." He knew what was best for his clients, because he listened to them and understood what they needed.

Now he's starting to create a strong social media presence and is working on developing an entirely new website for himself.

Rudy: He didn't have a website or social media presence before?

David: No, he wasn't doing it before. He was consistent on working his leads, his sphere of influence and building through that sphere of influence and then getting out there. He did buy into a lead-generation site, and he worked those leads like there was no tomorrow, like there was no food on the table and someone there had to close a deal. I think that's the energy and the drive that's required to make it to the top in this business.

Rudy: Dave and I shared a moment at a Tony Robbins seminar that brought a lot of things to light for me, and hopefully to a lot of the other people that were there. Tony asked us, "What if a doctor tells you tomorrow you're going to die in 30 days if you don't book $5,000,000 in volume. Here's what's going to end up happening. You would find a way to book that to avoid dying." That's the kind of energy and drive you need to be successful in this business. If you just want to go half measure, it's going to be a constant battle.

David: Let's talk about social media presence even though we're going to talk a little bit about it in a future chapter.

If you don't have a digital imprint, it's going to be very difficult to be trusted. I say that because if you don't have a website and you don't have a good social media presence as a real estate professional, then you will not be trusted as a local expert. Believe it or not, people will do research on you before they work with you.

Rudy: Look at the facts. The Millennials; anyone born after 1980, are a lot more tech-savvy and have access to more information than they did in the past. They are much more social, which is the way of the world now.

David: Online media is your digital billboard. You can put a billboard on a highway and thousands of people will pass by that billboard every day. But how many will call? Think of online media as a digital billboard. This is one they're actually looking at while they're on the highway and will complete a call to action.

Confidence: What Are You Really Selling?

Susan: Talk to us about confidence. What do agents need to know about confidence?

David: This is my favorite subject to talk about! You have to know your business and the product you're selling. In real estate, it's vital.

An agent who walks into a house in Miami, Florida without knowing the neighborhood—the schools, the price points, or the demographics of the neighborhood—is not going to know what to say when the seller asks, "What do you think my house can go for, and do you think it's important that X, Y, Z school is down the street?" When that happens, the agent's confidence level goes down the drain.

Knowing your market, knowing your job, knowing what you're doing, and knowing the house better than anyone else gives you confidence. Confidence is key in this business. If you walk through a door with your head down, and you really don't know what you're doing, you're in trouble right away.

Rudy: Yes, so do your homework.

David: Do your homework and know the neighborhood and market. Confidence is one of the most important things you can have to be successful. If you're not confident about an appointment you're about to go to, take someone with you who has the confidence, knowledge, and education to get the listing, and split the deal with that person. Do not be afraid to give up 50% of your deal, because 50% of something is better than 100% of nothing. If you walk into a meeting without the necessary confidence and education, you're going to fail. You want to talk about confidence, Rudy? You're the most confident person I know.

Talk about it from the title side. You're building your title company and your clients are real estate professionals. Who do you want to work with?

Rudy: I want to work with anyone who is motivated. On the title end, I don't necessarily only focus on top-hitting producers, even though they're obviously more appealing for a variety of reasons, some more obvious than others. I look at potential more than anything else, and I look at hunger, that eye-of-the-tiger type of thing only a few people have. That's important to me and I think it's important to the sellers. They want to work with people with passion and with conviction.

David: Those are skills you can absolutely develop. However, confidence comes with a couple things: prior successes and it also comes with education and knowledge. If you can walk into an appointment with a buyer who is viewing one of your listings, you should easily be able to answer questions like, *"What private schools are near this neighborhood?"* or *"Are the public schools any good?"* or *"What parks are close by?"*

If you have these answers, you're instantly confident about what you're selling. Confidence is a key feature when you're selling yourself because, at the end of the day, you're marketing real estate but people want to work with YOU. They want to work with you because they trust YOU and they like YOU. Those are the two main factors. They will trust you if you are confident their house can sell and you know the neighborhood.

For example, if a real estate agent has only ever sold $300,000 to $400,000 houses and now is connected through their network to someone who is selling a $2,000,000 house, what should the agent do? This agent has never sat in on a $2,000,000 appointment. My advice to that agent in that situation is don't walk in there without an agent who has already worked other $2 million deals. Find someone who can come along with you and split that one deal with that person.

This one deal is going to be a learning experience for you. Walk into that house or condo and say, "I brought my colleague with me so we can work together on selling your home. Let's talk about this." Now the pitch is not very different, but your confidence level goes through the roof, because you walked in with someone who knows the building, the neighborhood, the schools and the average price point, and who prepared with you prior to going to this appointment.

Susan: Do you think an agent just needs to do it for a single transaction, or how long do you think they need to partner with someone?

David: That's where the psychological part comes in, because it really depends on how long it takes for that particular person to get confident enough to handle it independently. I say to do it as many times as you need to. For some people, it's one time. They complete the transaction and say, "You know what? This wasn't as hard as I thought it was going to be, I was nervous for no reason." Other people may take three or four times. I say do it as many times as you absolutely need to until you get to where you need to be to handle it on your own.

Susan: It's a win-win for everyone. The new agent, the experienced agent, and the seller. They all win.

David: Exactly. You bring the business, and that agent brings the confidence and expertise. It's a win-win!

Marketing: Be Everywhere, All the Time!

Susan: Rudy, I think it was you who said, "Be everywhere all the time." Can you share what you mean by that?

Rudy: Actually that was Dave's comment, but he's seeing exactly what it is we're doing from a marketing and branding point. I think initially it extends from creating a particular type of brand. What's going to be the appeal? Who are we appealing to? Knowing your client is vital.

There are several steps before I can just jump into saying be everywhere every time, because there are prerequisites, and understanding what you're selling in this instance would be real estate. Understand the market you're selling to, because you have different markets and demographics, so understanding your buyer is important. From the marketing standpoint, once you've created a brand you think is appealing, then it is all about taking that brand and exposing it to as many avenues as you possibly can as much as possible.

David: Rudy has a very particular thing he does I enjoy. Rudy's client is ultimately the real estate agent. That's whom Rudy's going after. Step One, as Rudy said, is to understand your demographic and know who you're focusing on.

For a real estate agent, it's different. For a real estate agent, you're looking at maybe two buildings, or maybe you're looking at one neighborhood. Once you've established who you're going to go after, you can develop an "attack plan".

Rudy understands that his client is the agent; which is his demographic. There is no agent in Miami Dade County who doesn't know Nu World Title. There's a reason for that: He sponsors parties and charity events, anything a real estate professional will possibly attend. He's okay with having his name there, someway, somehow, so people remember it.

There's a reason there's a McDonald's every ten feet; with that branding, they know exactly where to open a store, and they know exactly what you're looking for, and they're giving you a product you want. When we say, "Be everywhere all the time," that's Rudy's model. When I ask agents where they want to farm, they tell me, "I want to farm downtown Miami." I tell them downtown Miami is a very big place, and have them choose maybe three buildings that they want to be a part of. "Okay, great. A, B, and C are the three buildings that I want to be a part of."

Now you're going to have to be everywhere all the time for those three buildings. Meaning, do you have a newsletter advertising it?

Are you sending postcards to the residents? Are you attending their board meetings, because those are open to the public? Are you visiting the concierge and letting them know that you're the expert in the building? Do you know the buildings? Do you know people who live there? Have you met them? Are you throwing parties for the building? You could ask the manager about hosting a breakfast party for the building and talk about what the market is like. Then potential sellers could sit down and learn about what their potential price could be for selling their homes.

You're there all the time. Now this is not an overnight success. Just because you sent some postcards and threw a party and you did it for one month, you can't expect massive response levels. It must be continuous over time.

Rudy: One of the key ingredients here is the way I look at my business, is to say, "What's going to make me unique and different? What's going to make someone want to work with me because essentially, we all do the same thing?" We're selling real estate or we're selling title, and I'm talking for the two people in this room. We do the exact same thing. There are hundreds and hundreds of us within our inner circle, surrounding areas, and community. Forget hundreds, there are thousands of us.

What's going to make us different and unique compared with the other thousands of agents out there?

The way you market and the quality and quantity in which you market will ultimately make a big difference. You don't want to continue to market the same way everyone else is doing it. You have to find a creative gene pool somewhere or at least reach out to someone who is a little bit more creative than you are and create a plan.

David: Then leverage it. Hire someone to do the creative for you. Here's the key. We're going to tell you to put 25% of your income into marketing so you can stay in everybody's face, and you do not do it short-term. This is a long-term goal. You can be the master at an area or specific type of client—whatever your focus is going to be: doctors, lawyers, attorneys, golf pros or football players? Whatever that focus is going to be, you need to go long-term on being there all the time. You are investing in yourself, but 90% of the readers of this book will not do it. This is the difference between the 10% of the people doing the majority of the business.

That's why Rudy has developed a huge business and surpassed so many agents. We've done it because we've been 100% consistent with being in everyone's face all the time.

Susan: How long do you think a new agent would take to sort of gain some traction in this?

Rudy: My opinion on sales in general is you create your own destiny. It's really on you how long it takes you to get traction.

David: I'll tell you this. The most you will hear is real estate agents in general take up to about six months to get into production. It could be as short as three months. What it boils down to is how much effort you put into your business, how much marketing you do and how much social media presence you have. Is your website well developed? Do you have a digital imprint? Are you networking with people? Are you out two or three times a week networking for business?

I once heard a story about a top broker in New York City. He told me that he would go to networking events with people he wanted to be around, but he couldn't afford those events. He would drink soda water so it looked like a drink because it was a Manhattan-priced drink, and they were $18 a glass. Now he's one of the top brokers in his area. Why? Because he continued to stay in everyone's face all the time and he never gave up. Now he goes to those same events and he has a real drink because he can afford it. In fact, now he can afford it for his whole team.

I can't tell you an exact time frame. I don't want to tell you you're going to be successful in six months. I don't want to tell you you're going to be successful in three months. What I will tell you is if you were to sit down with me and I give you a 90-day plan, you will be in production within 90 days. I didn't say rich. I said in production. If you keep that same plan going consistently, your production will only grow. The second you back off, your production fails.

David: You could be productive in 30 days.

Rudy: You could be productive in a day.

David: It just depends on how much you put into it.

Rudy: You could be productive prior to getting your license so you could start selling real estate right away.

David: I've had agents walk into my office for a job prior to their license. They would say, "I want to be a part of this. I read your article in *The Real Deal*. I read your article on *Curbed Miami*. I want to be a part of what you're developing here." I tell them, "Great. You can come to all the trainings. You can start learning, get the word out, but until you get licensed, you can't do any work."

They come to the trainings knowing they're getting ready, anticipating their license date. When they take the state exam and get the paper which says they passed, then they're ready to go. These are folks who are going to hit the ground running and put 110% into every single day in this business, understanding it's not easy, but it can be fruitful.

Susan: That's quite a commitment, versus someone who just sits back and is expecting the phone to ring.

David: Exactly. You can't just sit there and wait for the phone to ring. It's not going to happen.

Rudy: Remember, in real estate, just as with anything else, you're marketing everything that you represent. You're marketing a relationship, friendship and trust, an important component in this industry. You're also marketing reliability, and an extensive amount of other aspects, but I think those are probably the top priority with trust being number one.

David: You're selling yourself. You need to tell people that you are the right person for the job. When you do your marketing, it's not about the house. It really isn't. I love seeing those just-sold and just-listed houses. Great. Good job, Realtor. Tell me about you. What can you do for me?

Rudy: How am I going to be a "difference-maker"? What makes me unique? What makes me different?

I'll give you an example, and this is something that I've tried before. I like to think outside the box and be creative when it comes to getting in front of people in a fun and different way. I go to a football stadium here in Miami and during halftime or just prior to the start of the game, I take 1,000 business cards with me, and throw them all in the air from the upper deck. These 1,000 business cards floated throughout the entire stadium and I'm sure landed in 1,000 people's seats! Did I expect any traction or business from it *per se*? No, but I got my name out there. I furthered my brand. I exposed myself to more people.

That's part of marketing. It's one example, and I'm sure you could do that in a lot of different sports venues. It's a gathering where a lot of people are in one particular moment in time. If you can maximize your potential from a branding, marketing standpoint, why not do it? Get creative with it. It worked out, and I did get some phone calls. Some real estate agents called to say, "This is pretty brave of you, and unique, and we liked it!"

Susan: That's awesome. Let's face it; business cards can be pretty cheap to print these days.

Rudy: I also believe in giving back to the community. I think it's the right thing to do. Not just to create a certain brand and expose your brand even more in a good light. It's a different type of deal for me because my company and I enjoy helping charities, giving back, and helping the less fortunate. When you do this, it puts you in a good light with the community.

David: What Rudy is also saying, and it's something I always tell my agents, you must come from a place of contribution. If you're not coming from a place of contribution, then you're not genuine.

For example, if you live in the Coconut Grove community, you could join the Chamber of Commerce to network with other businesses that come together to help the community. Again, find a charity in the local area; maybe there's a hospital in the area with a children's cancer center you could help. You're giving back. Like Rudy says, giving back to the community that you profit from is so important.

The whole picture might look like this. You develop your foundation maybe social media and focusing on the areas you want to farm. Then you door-knock those houses, actively being present in their communities.

You're part of the charities in their communities, attend their community meetings. It all ties together.

Then next step is to reinvest 25% of your income back to your marketing. Now you have radio spots that play in the community, TV ads that run on local channels, newspapers and print magazines.

Rudy: Basically any outlet that will allow you to be visible. I think Dave covered every single one of them just now.

David: Is there a baseball team, a kid's softball team around? What if you were the sponsor? Not only did you help that team get all the uniforms they needed, but you're also in everybody's face again.

Susan: These aren't hard things to do and sound fun. This is not drudgery or having to go to networking events or shaking hands and forcing yourself out there. These ideas are exciting and fresh.

Rudy: That's what I'm talking about. Do something crazy. Throw 1,000 cards and see what happens.

Social Media: How Important Is This to Your Business?

Susan: I know we just touched on it briefly earlier, but how important is social media to today's real estate agent?

David: Social media is your digital billboard. Period, end of story. There are so many social media platforms out there. This is an opportunity for you to be in everyone's face. I can throw 100 statistics at you, but let's face it, almost everyone has a social media account. There are more than seven billion people on the planet. Three-and-a-half billion of them have social media accounts. Almost half of the people in the entire world have social media accounts. People are spending close to an hour and a half on average worldwide on social media every day. They're checking Facebook, Twitter, YouTube, and watching videos. It's so important you maintain a strong social media presence, because social media's going to be stronger than your website.

A lot of people think if they have a website, they're good. That's wrong. Starbucks, for instance, has 1.8 million people visit their website yearly. But! They have 18 million people visit their social media landing page, their business page. There's a huge difference.

Social media is where people get their news, where they understand what's going on in the community. They see everything on social media. The Millennial is not watching TV News anymore. No one reads the newspaper. When was the last time you bought a newspaper? Maybe some people like the feel of a newspaper in their hands. I don't. I want to read my news on my phone. I can often get through my entire social media feed with so many people posting news articles that I'll know exactly what's going on in the world. I can click the link and read it.

Social media is your digital billboard. It is your opportunity, an opportunity the generation behind us did not have. In order for the generation behind us to get in front of people, they had to visit them. They had breakfasts and lunches all day long, meeting after meeting and a lot of time on the telephone.

Now you have an opportunity to post one post on social media and get in front of 5,000 people instantly. This is your reach. This is an opportunity, when we say be everywhere all the time; this is your opportunity to be in Paris, Belgium, or Brazil while sitting in Miami. Why? Because you can create social media ads, which focus on a country, an area or a certain price point. It is the opportunity for you to grow your business to unbelievable heights by being in front of everybody at all times.

Susan: Do you have to spend a lot of money to do that?

David: You don't. For the most part, social media sites are free to use. That's one of the most amazing things about it. The only time you spend money is when you start to advertise with them. Let me tell you something. An advertisement on Facebook is a lot cheaper than an advertisement anywhere else. Period. If you want to purchase a full-page ad in a magazine, you're looking at $1,800. They send out that magazine and maybe the person reading the magazine looks at your ad, maybe they don't. Maybe half of those magazines never even get picked up. They just sit on the table at the doctor's office, or wherever it is they sit. Maybe no one ever sees your ad, but if you spent $30 on Facebook ad, you could be in front of thousands of people easily and instantly, and you can target who actually is going to see it. It's important to have the foundation social media provides.

Susan: What do you mean when you say you can target who sees it, David?

David: On Facebook, for example, you can target people by location, zip code, city, or by age range. You want people who are going to be buying or selling in that neighborhood, so maybe it's from 25 to 45 or maybe it's from 45 to 65, depending on the neighborhood.

You can focus on median income or specific interests. You can even focus on people who are interested in real estate and who have indicated on their social media that they like real estate. Then only those people in your target criteria see your advertisement. Here's another news flash people don't realize. When you advertise with Facebook, it automatically advertises on Instagram because Facebook owns Instagram. This kind of activity instantly builds your online presence.

People need to build at least the bare minimum of a foundation on social media, which is a Facebook business page, an Instagram business page, a Twitter account, a YouTube channel and a LinkedIn account. The other Social Media platforms are important, as well, but those five are the foundation. That's where the majority of people are. LinkedIn is a business model. It's where your resume is and you can connect with other business professionals. Twitter is your news feed where you can spread news about what's happening in the market you serve. The majority of businesses and large corporations have a Twitter to connect with their consumers.

Facebook is the largest platform out there. Not only is it the largest, with the most users, it is the largest marketing company in the world and they develop no marketing material.

You build it all for them and then pay them to put it in their algorithm. Instagram is your picture window to your business. It shows live beautiful photos of everything you are doing. I am finding that many agents are beginning to earn a lot of business off having amazing Instagram accounts with vibrant photos of gorgeous homes.

YouTube is owned by Google. If you're putting videos up on YouTube, you're getting a boost by Google and Google+. Not only that, but people will spend on average an hour-and-a-half watching video per day. If I want to find out anything I need to know about anything—like how to make cold calls—I can YouTube it.

Here's the crazy part. People are moving closer to YouTube. The number one search engine in the world? Google. Number two? YouTube. Why? People Google everything. Everybody says, "Google that." Going back to the cold call example, if I want to make a really good cold call, I'll Google it. When I Google it, because Google owns YouTube, there are going to be some videos on there. I'll click on YouTube, and I might be able to watch professional real estate agents who are very, very good at cold calling making some calls. I can sit there and learn what they're doing on the spot.

Susan: Again, that doesn't cost any money.

David: It's all free. You can create videos that speak to your client base. Educate them about the community, talk about anything that's going on or create live videos.

When you do this, you're coming from a place of contribution, as well. You're not just saying, "Look at this house that sold, look at that house that sold." In turn, you also have videos on houses you're listing and you are responsible for selling. These videos can be searched and people can have a tour of the house without even being there. There are times you can sell the house to someone in another country because they saw the video and loved the house.

Business Partners and Alliances

Susan: Talk to us about business partners and alliances.

David: As a real estate professional, it's extremely important to align yourself with business professionals who are going to treat your clients the way you treat your clients. You align yourself with the right people because you never want to refer a client to someone who's going to do a bad job.

Rudy: The core of the matter is simple. Every real estate agent just doesn't sell a home and get paid a commission. Every transaction entails third party vendors like an appraisal company, a title agency or attorney and a mortgage loan officer if there's financing involved. You can't do it alone.

David: Good point. As a real estate professional, you're a consultant to your client. Your client is going to come to you and ask, "Do you have a lender? Do you have a great title company or escrow company? Do you have a good real estate attorney? Do you have a good home inspector? Do you have a pool guy? Do you have a maintenance guy? Do you have a yard guy? Do you have a roofer?"

In this business, you want to align yourself with great professionals who are going to maintain a high standard, because it will reflect on you. You want to build those business relationships so you continue to work together to grow your business, which in turn helps grow their businesses. They become your business partners, allies and team. I hate to say it like this, but like the Avengers. That's a team with different powers and purposes, which come from different worlds, but as a team they serve one amazing purpose.

Rudy: All to provide the best possible experience to your clients.

David: Exactly. When I, David Kurz at Kurz Real Estate, tell someone, "Don't worry, I have the best title company, I have the best escrow company in town," and I say, "This is Rudy Hernandez from Nu World Title," they know that because of the service I've provided them thus far, whoever I refer them to, they're going to trust. That person is going to then, in turn, give them a great experience. It's very important to have those types of alliances in your business because you're not just an agent, you're a consultant. You're a trusted person now. People are using you because they trust you. You need to make sure you have outlets for your clients for everything they may possibly need.

If you don't, go find what you need from one of your current business partners - who they may know and refer.

Susan: There are people out there who can make your life easier and better and make you look good. Connect with those people and build a team around you.

David: You must build your business so that you are the real consultant. You align yourself with people who understand and provide the same level of customer service that you do or above.

The Close: If You Don't Ask, You Will Not Receive

Susan: Let's talk about what you mean by "If you don't ask, you will not receive."

David: I believe everything in real estate is a close. If someone refers business to me, and says, "Hey, my cousin Vicky wants to buy a house." When I call Vicky, if I'm able to set an appointment with her, that's one close. At the appointment, if I'm able to convince her I'm the right person to help her purchase her house, that's another close. When we're searching for houses, and she chooses the right one, because I was able to show her exactly what she asked for, that's another close. If you get to the closing table, that's the real close, the one that pays the commission.

I believe through every part of the process, there's a close involved. However, if you don't ask for the close, you will not receive it. I have a story about a coach I met that does sales trainings with large corporations. He asked me, "What do you do at the closing table when someone buys a house with you?" I said, "I bring them a bottle of wine, a couple wine glasses and a gift. I congratulate them, and join them for the celebration of their transaction."

I take a picture with them, and put it on my social media platforms to let everybody know we closed another house.

He said, "Oh, that's great. How did that bring you more business?" I said, "Well it didn't, but maybe someone on social media sees I'm closing homes and they call me." He said, "This is what I want you to do at your next closing. I want you to sit across the table when they're all done and they're in euphoria because they just bought a home or they just sold one and put a lot of money in the bank. Now they might be off to buy another home with you. They've accomplished their mission. You helped them get there." He said, "Look at them across the table and say, 'Are you 110% happy with the service I provided you?' 'Yes I am. Thank you so much for helping us get into our beautiful home. You're the best; amazing!' 'Do you know anyone looking to buy or sell real estate right now?'"

Then stop talking, and allow them the opportunity to answer you. Don't continue to convince them you're the right person. You are the right person! You just helped them close on their home. You're the right person, there's no need to convince them, but you have to ask for the business. If you don't ask for the business, you will not get the business.

From the beginning of the phone call, you say, "Hi Liz, how are you? I was referred to you..." so forth, so on, and that phone call needs to end with, "When can we meet?" That's the close for that phone call. When you're at the table and you sit down with them, the last question is, "When can we go look at houses? How's Tuesday?" That's the close.

When they go to the house, you say, "Is this house everything you dreamed of?" "Yes, it is." "What would stop you from placing an offer right now?" Don't talk and allow them the opportunity to answer you. That's another close. When you get them to the closing table, they close on their house, and you ask them for referral business. That's another close, but if you don't ask these multiple questions, you will not get the business you deserve.

Susan: This is what separates an average agent from one who is always selling. Great stuff!

How to Get Started Today Building Your Successful Real Estate Business

Susan: If someone's interested in joining your company, David, what is the process you take them through?

David: First let me share that we are already working on our next book! Now that you know about what it takes to be a real estate agent and you understand there's a blueprint in effect and you have to follow those who have already done it. You are now ready for our next book which is going to cover the four points of the foundation of developing this blueprint.

I want to teach you the foundation to develop your real estate business, so we can build the house in future books. The four points are your personal network, your website presence, your social media presence, and your print presence. In the next book, we're going to talk about putting all four of those into effect, and then showing you how they all intermix and lead in one direction, which is lead generation and success.

Susan: It will go even deeper into some of the topics we talked about in this book?

David: Exactly, so the next book is going to be the Blueprint Two, The Foundation to Marketing and Selling Today.

Susan: If an agent reading this is interested in joining your company, talk to us about the process you take them through.

David: If an agent decides to join Kurz Real Estate, one of the benefits they're going to receive is one-on-one connection. My mission is to spend at least 30 minutes to an hour with every new agent, so we can develop the first 90 days of business. It doesn't matter if you're a brand new agent, a mid-level successful agent or if you're a super-successful agent. When you join Kurz Real Estate, we're sitting down together and we're coming up with the next 90 days of your business, and we're putting those four-points into action. We're going to figure out what it is you're passionate about and good at, and then we're going to turn that into a real estate business for you.

That's what makes us different; we have an open space, collaborative environment. We've created a culture in which we don't keep any secrets from each other. We all want to succeed, and we all want to do it together. We've created an open and collaborative environment in our office that allows our agents to work together and grow their businesses individually or as part of a team.

Many real estate companies will offer you training. We do that, as well. What many real estate companies don't offer you is follow-up and accountability on the training they gave you. They'll give you a plethora of training and expect you to go out and do this by yourself. We're not doing that here at Kurz Real Estate. At Kurz Real Estate, we want to give you the training, the blueprint, the map, and we want to hold you accountable for following the lead.

Susan: Where can prospective agents go for more information?

David: They can call us directly at **786-529-5273**. They can visit our website at **www.KurzRealEstate.com** or they can e-mail us at **JoinTheMovement@KurzRE.com**.

They can do searches on social media for Kurz Real Estate. We're **@KurzRealEstate** on Facebook, **@KurzRealEstate** on Instagram, and they can search for **#JOINTheMovement** for any activity in regards to recruiting.

Susan: I want to thank you both. I think what you've done here is laid out. That you can't just get your real estate license, sit back and wait for success. You must go after it.

Everything you've shared with us today can be done easily; it's not like you're asking them to write a check for $10,000 to get a marketing and PR campaign going. It may take work, but, as you pointed out, that's what differentiates the 10% from the 90% of agents.

David: It's all about taking action, grassroots, brass knuckles, getting out there and getting it done.

Susan: Thank you both for sharing with us. I can't wait to see the next book, too!

David: We can't either. Thank you so much, Susan and Rudy, always a pleasure.

Rudy: Don't forget: Be everywhere, all the time! Thanks, Susan and David!

Here's How to Build Your Successful Real Estate Business

For a real estate agent, going from a few transactions a year to multiple deals a month takes more than just hard work. You need to have the right mindset and team supporting you. Most real estate companies claim they offer their agents training and support. But when you look a little closer, the training is not tailored to the things you struggle with.

That's where we come in. When you join Kurz Real Estate, we sit down one on one and put together a 90-day action plan to help you turn your real estate practice into a successful business.

Step 1: We work with you to figure out what you're passionate about and use that to turn it into a business you fall in love with. No longer will you dread trying to drum up business. Business will be coming to you.

Step 2: Once we understand how you work best, we work with you one-on-one during your first 90 days putting our four-point action plan to work for you. Although we work with a blueprint, it is tailored to your unique abilities and talent.

Step 3: You get to tap into our network and work in a truly collaborative environment. Gone are the days of you working in the corner by yourself. Benefit from having the support you need to do your best work.

Most REALTORS are sitting on a gold mine if they just knew how to become the center of influence for their network.

Now you can stop chasing business and put a plan in place to let it come to you.

If you'd like us to help, send an email to: JoinTheMovement@KurzRE.com and we'll take it

www.ingramcontent.com/pod-product-compliance
Lightning Source LLC
Chambersburg PA
CBHW070135210526
45170CB00013B/1088